REVISED EDITION

HAROLD PRINCE
in association with RUTH MITCHELL
presents

# PACIFIC OVERTURES

starring

## MAKO

with

## SOON-TECK OH

### YUKI SHIMODA   SAB SHIMONO   ISAO SATO

ALVIN ING • ERNEST HARADA • JAMES DYBAS • MARK HSU SYERS • PATRICK KINSER-LAU

Music and Lyrics by
# STEPHEN SONDHEIM

Book by
# JOHN WEIDMAN

Additional material by
## HUGH WHEELER

| Scenic production designed by | Costumes designed by | Lighting designed by |
|---|---|---|
| **BORIS ARONSON** | **FLORENCE KLOTZ** | **THARON MUSSER** |
| Orchestrations by | Musical direction by | Dance Music by |
| **JONATHAN TUNICK** | **PAUL GEMIGNANI** | **DANIEL TROOB** |
| Kabuki consultant | Make-up & Wigs designed by | Masks & Dolls by |
| **HARUKI FUJIMOTO** | **RICHARD ALLEN** | **E. J. TAYLOR** |

Music Publisher
**TOMMY VALANDO**

Choreography by
## PATRICIA BIRCH

Production directed by
# HAROLD PRINCE

Music administrator for Mr. Sondheim: Sean Patrick Flahaven, Warner/Chappell Music

This edition has been prepared, following the wishes of Stephen Sondheim, from the final, revised composer's score. It differs in many ways from the original edition of the vocal score. Small discrepancies may be found between it and orchestral parts. Insofar as discrepancies in the lyrics, this vocal score is to be considered correct.

Live dramatic performance rights for "Pacific Overtures" are represented exclusively by
Music Theatre International (MTI)
421 West 54th Street, New York, NY 10019.
www.MTIshows.com
For further information, please call (212) 541-4684
or email: Licensing@MTIshows.com

ISBN 978-1-4234-7288-9

# RILTING MUSIC, INC.

EXCLUSIVELY DISTRIBUTED BY

7777 W. BLUEMOUND RD. P.O. BOX 13819 MILWAUKEE, WI 53213

For all works contained herein:
Unauthorized copying, arranging, adapting, recording, Internet posting, public performance,
or other distribution of the printed music in this publication is an infringement of copyright.
Infringers are liable under the law.

Visit Hal Leonard Online at
**www.halleonard.com**

PREMIER PERFORMANCE AT THE WINTER GARDEN THEATRE
NEW YORK, JANUARY 11, 1976

## CAST OF CHARACTERS
(In Order of Appearance)

Reciter .................................................................................................................Mako
Abe, First Councillor ...............................................................................Yuki Shimoda
Manjiro...................................................................................................Sab Shimono
Second Councillor...................................................................................James Dybas
Shogun's Mother ...........................................................................................Alvin Ing
Third Councillor......................................................................................... Freddy Mao
Kayama ...................................................................................................... Isao Sato
Tamate (Kayama's Wife)
Samurai
Storyteller .............................................................Soon-Teck Oh
Swordsman
Samurai............................................................ Ernest Abuba, Mark Hsu Syers
Servant ................................................................................ Haruki Fujimoto
Observers................................................................... Alvin Ing, Ricardo Tobia
Fisherman...............................................................................Jae Woo Lee
Merchant................................................................................... Alvin Ing
Son .................................................................................... Timm Fujii
Grandmother .................................................................... Conrad Yama
Thief .............................................................................. Mark Hsu Syers
Adams..................................................................................Ernest Abuba
Williams ............................................................................... Larry Hama
Commodore Matthew Calbraith Perry...................................... Haruki Fujimoto
Shogun's Wife....................................................................... Freda Foh Shen
Physician ......................................................................... Ernest Harada
Priests.............................................................Timm Fujii, Gedde Watanabe
Soothsayer ...................................................................... Mark Hsu Syers
Sumo Wrestlers .................................................... Conrad Yama, Jae Woo Lee
Shogun's Companion ................................................Patrick Kinser-Lau
Shogun.......................................................................................Mako
Madam...................................................................... Ernest Harada
Girls............................................................ Timm Fujii, Patrick Kinser-Lau,
Gedde Watanabe, Leslie Watanabe
Old Man...................................................................... James Dybas
Boy.............................................................................. Gedde Watanabe
Warrior ...................................................................... Mark Hsu Syers
Imperial Priest ......................................................................Tom Matsusaka
Nobles.............................................................Ernest Abuba, Timm Fujii
American Admiral................................................................. Alvin Ing
British Admiral............................................................. Ernest Harada
Dutch Admiral....................................................Patrick Kinser-Lau
Russian Admiral ...................................................... Mark Hsu Syers
French Admiral ......................................................................James Dybas
Lords of the South............................................... Larry Hama, Jae Woo Lee
Jonathan Goble ...............................................................................Mako
Japanese Merchant............................................................ Conrad Yama
Samurai's Daughter............................................................... Freddy Mao
British Sailors.........................Timm Fujii, Patrick Kinser-Lau, Mark Hsu Syers
Proscenium Servants, Sailors, and Townspeople ...Susan Kikuchi, Diane Lam,
Kim Miyori, Freda Foh Shen, Kenneth S. Eiland, Timm Fujii, Joey Ginza,
Patrick Kinser-Lau, Tony Marinyo, Kevin Maung, Dingo Secretario,
Mark Hsu Syers, Ricardo Tobia, Gedde Watanabe, Leslie Watanabe
Musicians.............................Fusako Yoshida (Shamisen), Genji Ito (Percussion)

PLACE: Japan

TIME: Act One—July, 1853
Act Two—From then on

## MUSICAL NUMBERS

### ACT ONE

### ACT TWO

### INSTRUMENTATION

Reed 1: Flute, Piccolo, Alto Flute, Recorder; Reed 2: Flute, Piccolo, B♭ Clarinet, E♭ Clarinet; Reed 3: B♭ Clarinet, Bass Clarinet, Flute; Reed 4: Bassoon, B♭ Clarinet; 2 Horns, 2 Trumpets, 1 Trombone, 2 Percussion, 1 Harp, 1 Keyboard, 4 Violins, 2 Violas, 2 Cellos, 1 Bass plus Stage Band: Shamisen, Shakuhachi, Drums, etc.

**The purchase of this score does not constitute permission to perform. Applications for performance of this work, whether legitimate, stock, amateur, or foreign should be addressed to the licensing agent.**

**STEPHEN SONDHEIM** wrote the music and lyrics for *Road Show* (2008), *Passion* (1994), *Assassins* (1991), *Into the Woods* (1987), *Sunday in the Park with George* (1984), *Merrily We Roll Along* (1981), *Sweeney Todd* (1979), *Pacific Overtures* (1976), *The Frogs* (1974), *A Little Night Music* (1973), *Follies* (1971, revised in London, 1987), *Company* (1970), *Anyone Can Whistle* (1964), and *A Funny Thing Happened on the Way to the Forum* (1962), as well as lyrics for *West Side Story* (1957), *Gypsy* (1959), *Do I Hear A Waltz?* (1965), and additional lyrics for *Candide* (1973). *Side by Side by Sondheim* (1976), *Marry Me A Little* (1981), *You're Gonna Love Tomorrow* (1983), and *Putting It Together* (1992) are anthologies of this work as a composer and lyricist. For films, he composed the scores of *Stavisky* (1974) and *Reds* (1981) and songs for *Dick Tracy* (1990), for which he won an Academy Award. He also wrote songs for the television production "Evening Primrose" (1966), co-authored the film *The Last of Sheila* (1973) and the play *Getting Away With Murder* (1996), and provided incidental music for the plays *The Girls of Summer* (1956), *Invitation to a March* (1961), and *Twigs* (1971). He won Tony Awards for Best Score for a Musical for *Passion*, *Into the Woods*, *Sweeney Todd*, *A Little Night Music*, *Follies*, and *Company*. All of these shows won the New York Drama Critics Circle Award, as did *Pacific Overtures* and *Sunday in the Park with George*, the latter also receiving the Pulitzer Prize for Drama (1985). He received a special 2008 Tony Award for Lifetime Achievement in the Theatre. Mr. Sondheim was born in 1930 and raised in New York City. He graduated from Williams College, winning the Hutchinson Prize for Music Composition, after which he studied theory and composition with Milton Babbitt. He is on the Council of the Dramatists Guild, the national association of playwrights, composers, and lyricists, having served as its president from 1973 to 1981, and in 1983 was elected to the American Academy of Arts and Letters. In 1990 he was appointed the first Visiting Professor of Contemporary Theatre at Oxford University and in 1993 was a recipient of the Kennedy Center Honors.

*for Hal Prince*

# PACIFIC OVERTURES
## Act I Prelude

Music and Lyrics by
STEPHEN SONDHEIM

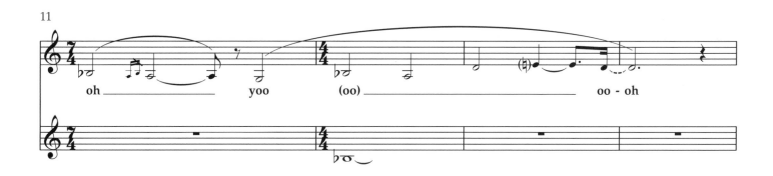

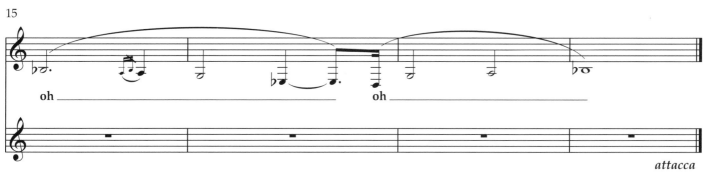

*attacca*
Stage Drums

Copyright © 1975, 1976 (Renewed), 1979 RILTING MUSIC, INC.
All Rights Administered by WB MUSIC CORP.
All Rights Reserved   Used by Permission

# The Advantages of Floating
# in the Middle of the Sea

(Reciter, Company)

**No. 1**

*Cue: A STAGEHAND runs the show curtain across the stage, revealing the cast.*

**Moderato**

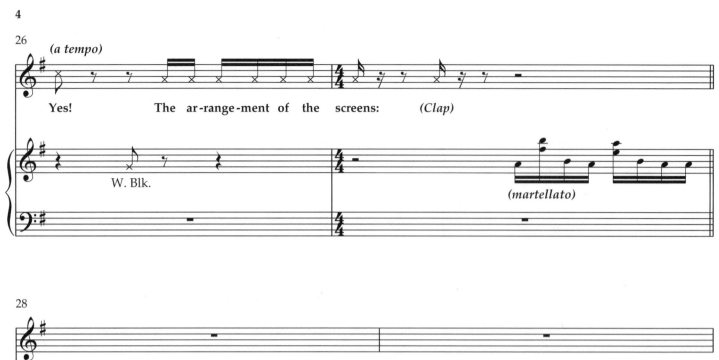

Yes! The ar-range-ment of the screens: *(Clap)*

We

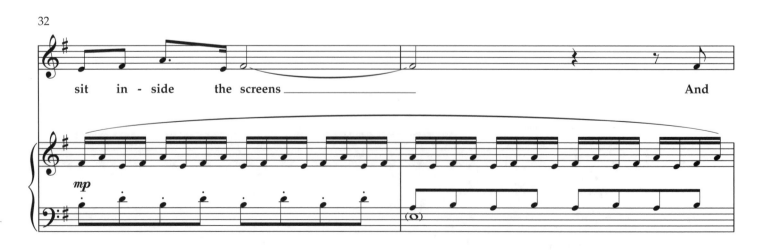

sit in - side the screens _____ And

42

scenes of screens like the ones that glide._____ And

44

no one press - es in,_____ And

46

no one glanc - es out,_____ And

48

kings are burn - ing some - where._____ Not

cresc.

ALL:

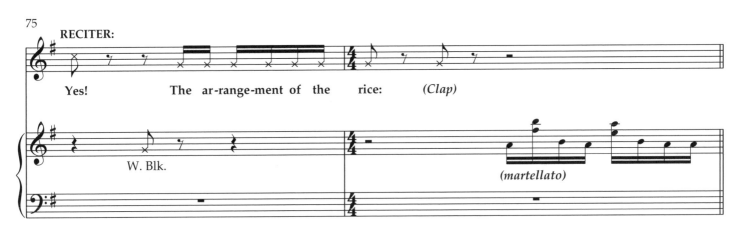

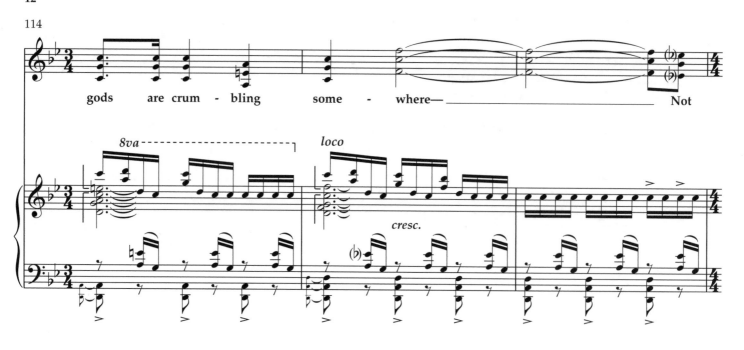

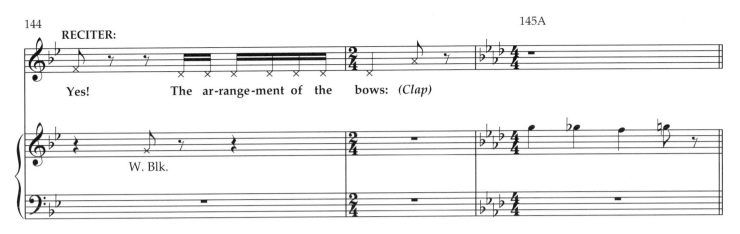

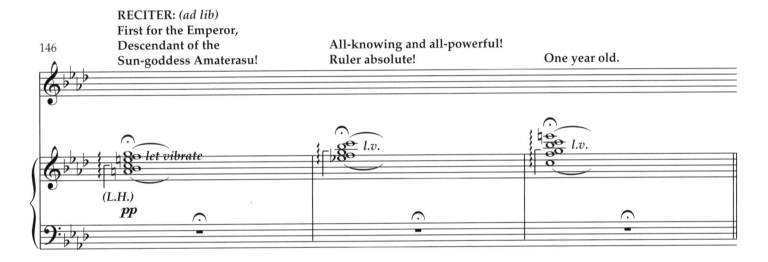

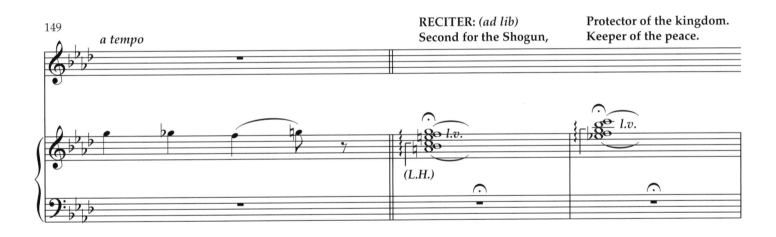

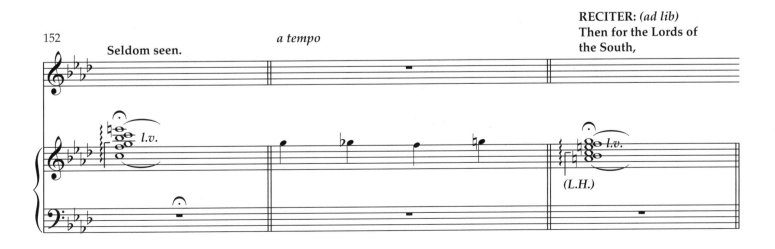

155

**Vassals to the Shogun,
Loyal to their master...**

**Not for long.**

[To bar 196]

And

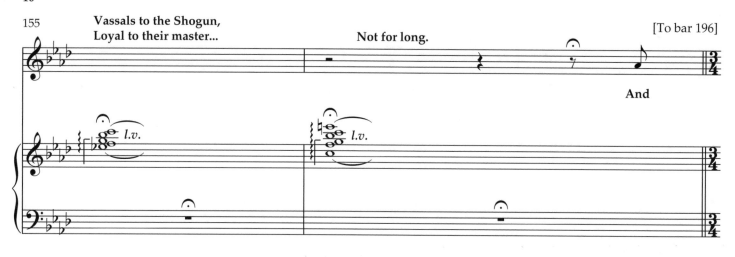

196

*rit.* *accel.* ALL:

kings are burn - ing some - where. _____ Not

199

*a tempo*

ALL: *(last time)*

here!

The ad -

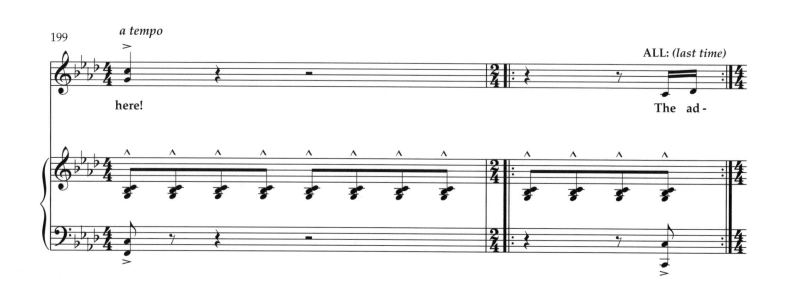

201

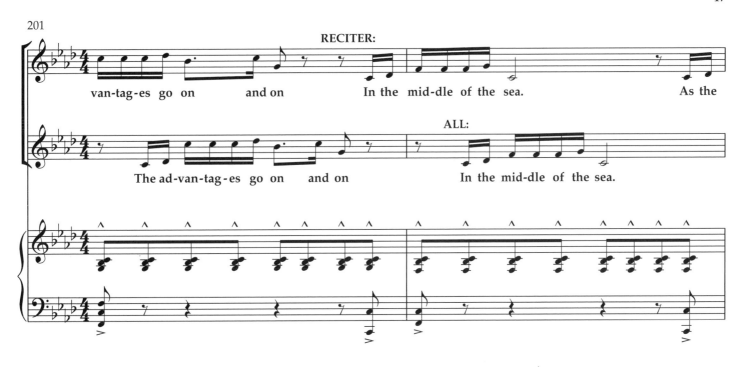

203

205

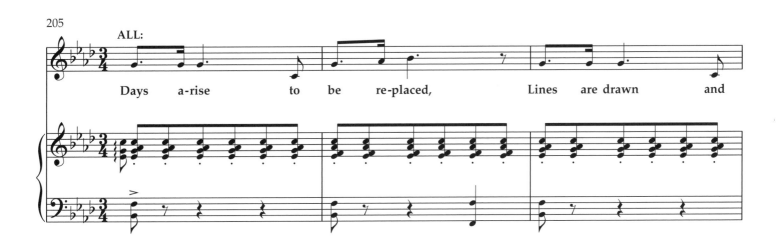

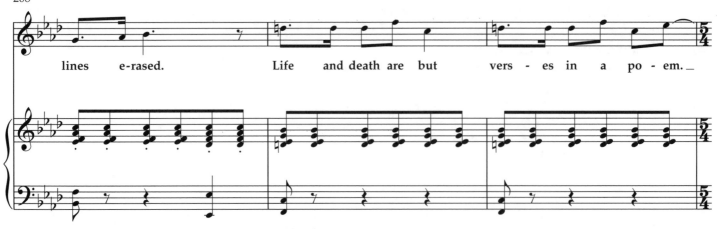

lines e-rased. Life and death are but vers - es in a po - em. __

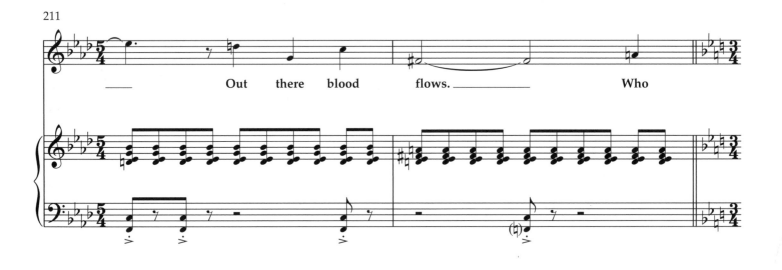

__ Out there blood flows. _____ Who

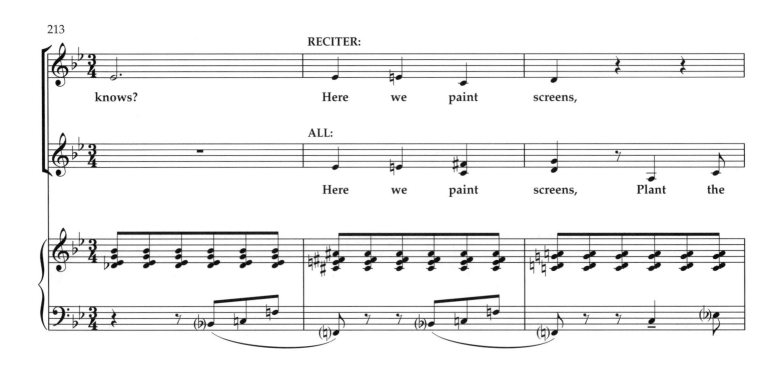

knows?

RECITER:
Here we paint screens,

ALL:
Here we paint screens, Plant the

20

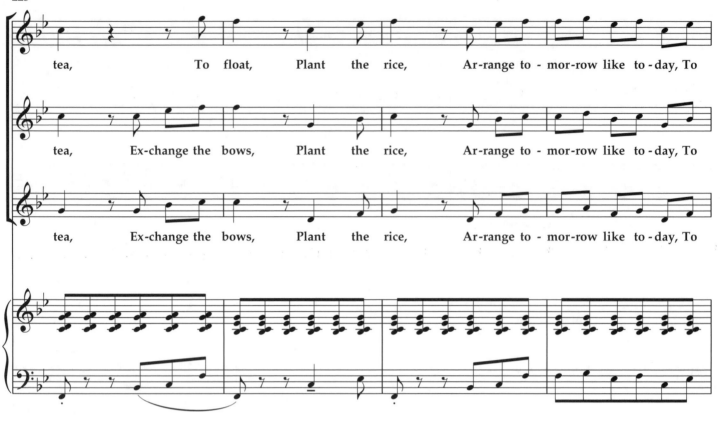

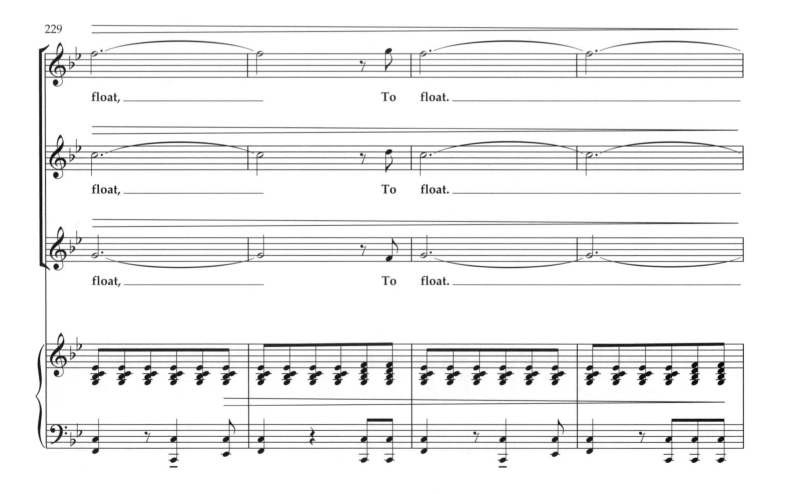

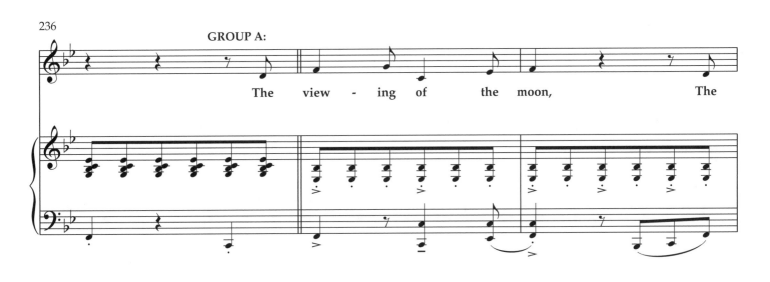

GROUP A:

The view - ing of the moon, The

plant - ing of the rice, The stir - ring of the tea, The

RECITER:

We float.

# No. 2      Prayers - Underscore

*Cue:* ABE: ... may the Gods of our fathers make you equal to this awesome task.

TAMATE: What did the
councilors say? *etc.*

*[Slow segue to
"TAMATE'S DANCE" No. 3]*

# No. 3

# Tamate's Dance - There Is No Other Way

### (Two Observers)

*Cue:* **KAYAMA: The Americans are here.**

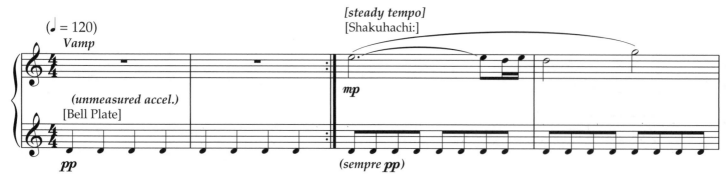

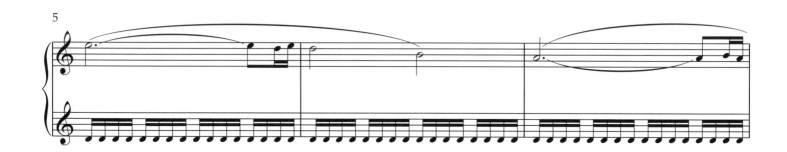

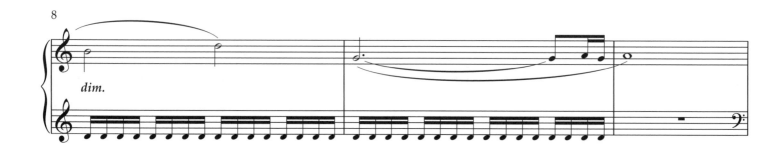

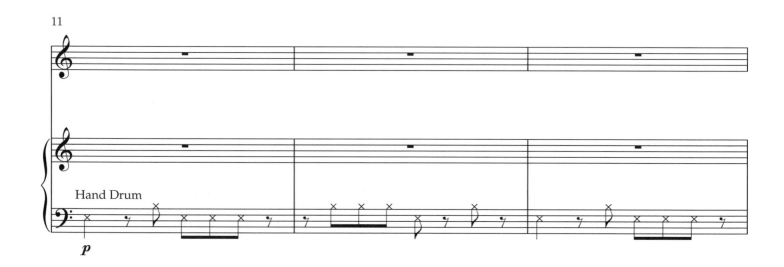

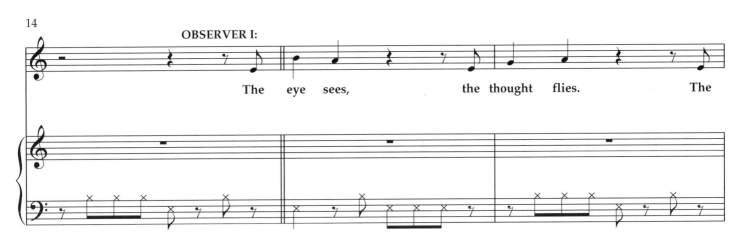

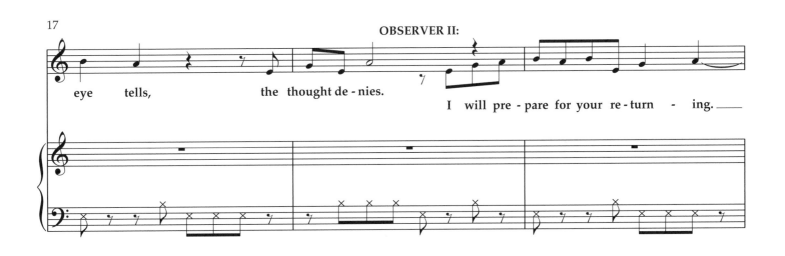

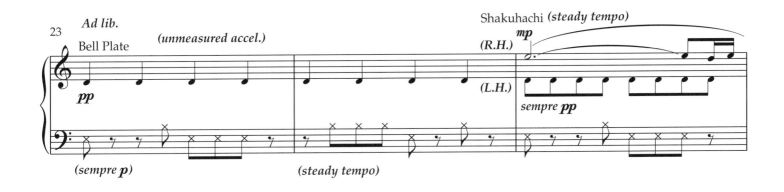

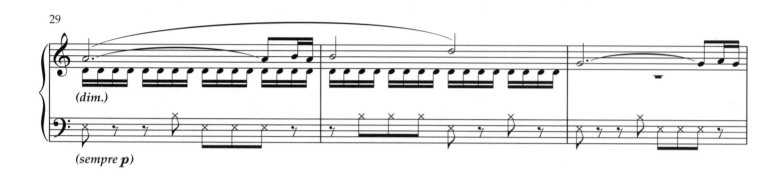

OBSERVER I:

The

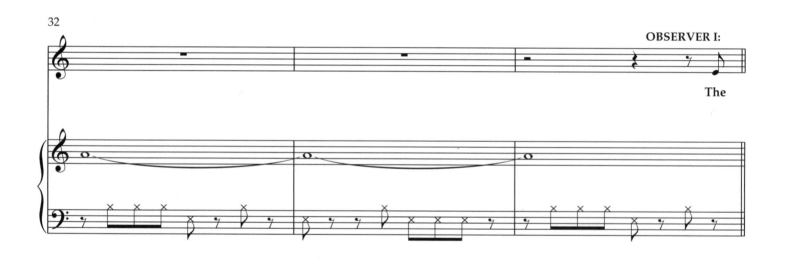

word   falls,        the  heart   cries.        The  heart  knows        the

*gliss.*

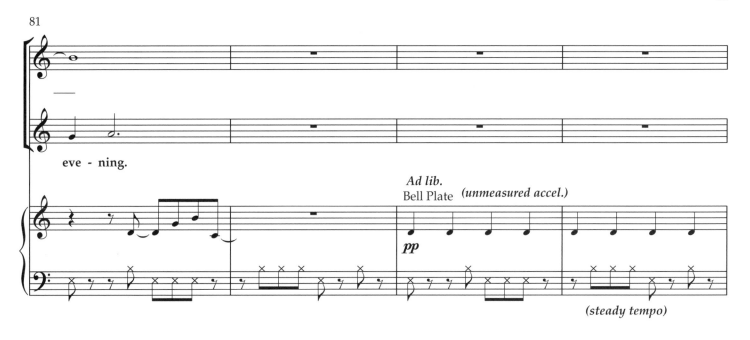

eve - ning.

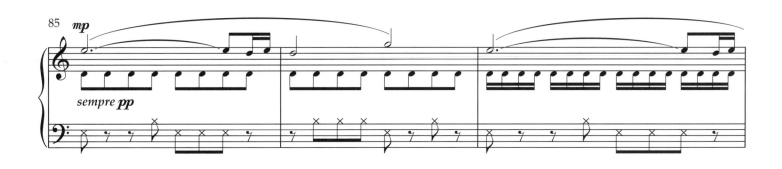

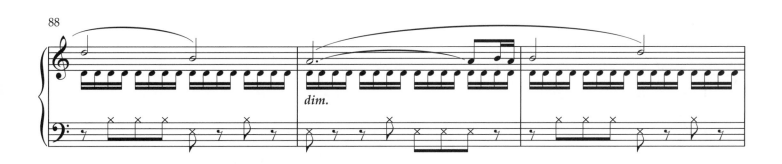

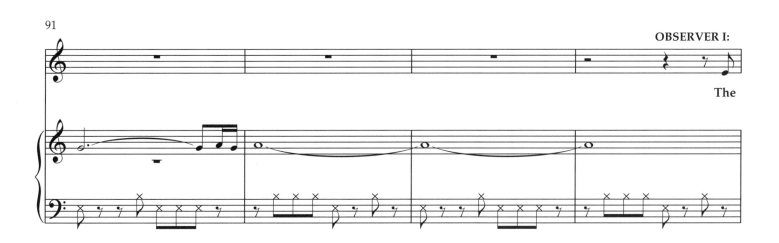

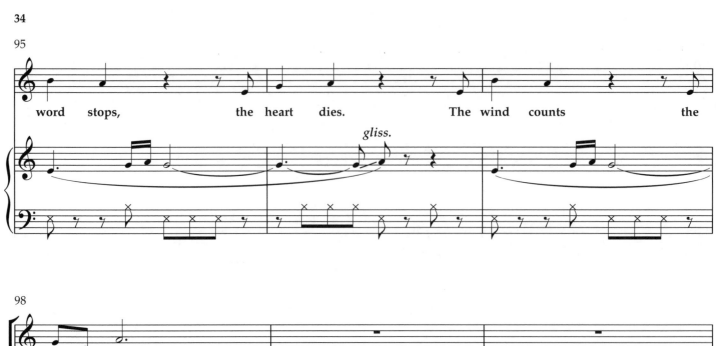

word stops, the heart dies. The wind counts the

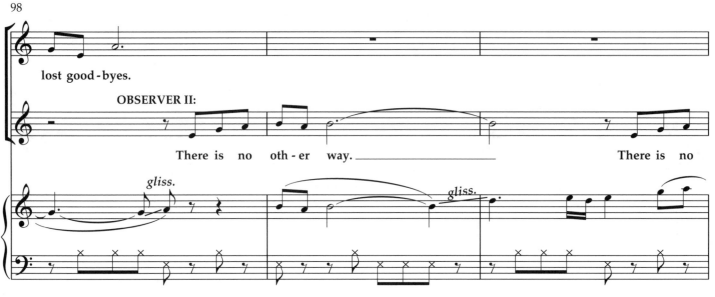

lost good-byes.

OBSERVER II:

There is no oth-er way. _____ There is no

oth-er way. _____

(Drums continue)

*(unmeasured accel.)*

Bell Plate

*pp*

*(sempre pp)*

*(Drum)*

[Segue to No. 4]

# No. 4

# Four Black Dragons
### (Fisherman, Thief, Reciter, Chorus)

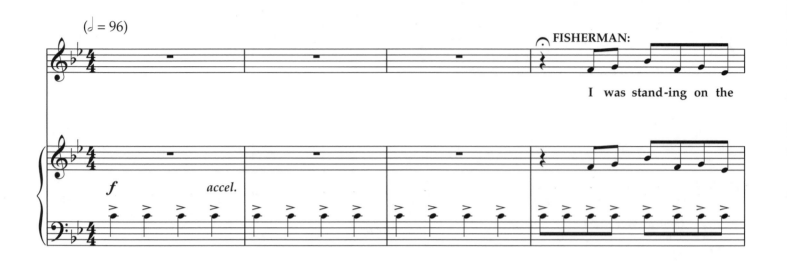

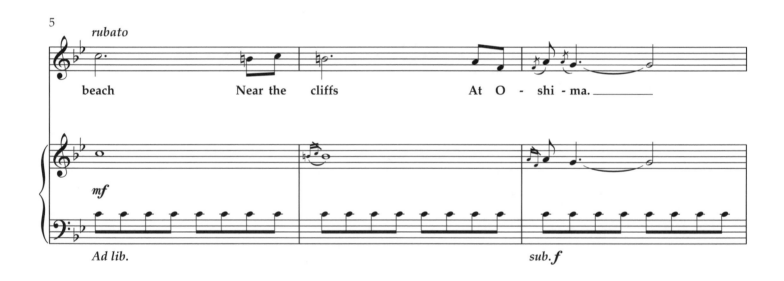

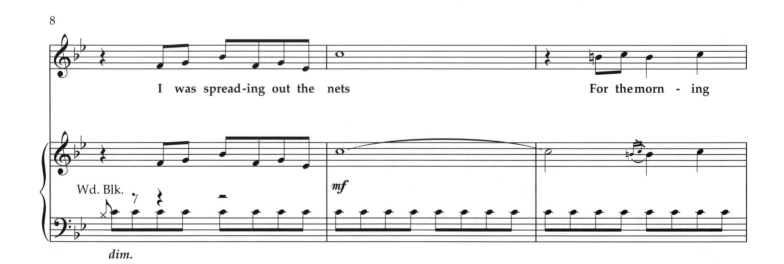

RECITER: Confucius tells the story of... *etc.*  [To bar 51S]

52E

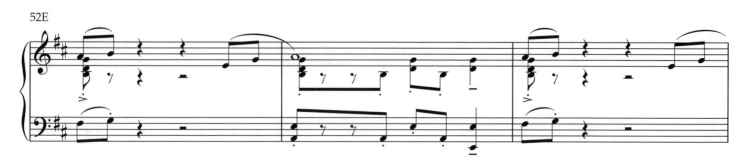

52H

Vamp        *[a thief enters]*

52L                          53

**THIEF:**

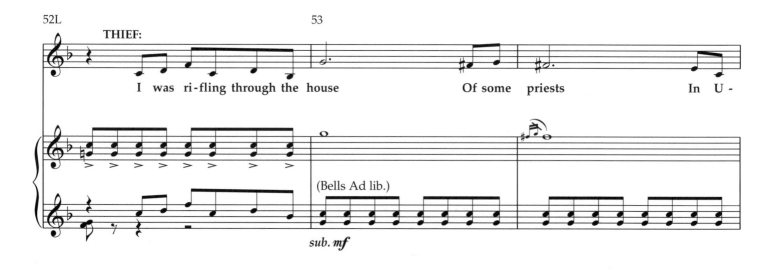

I    was   ri-fling through the house       Of some   priests        In  U-

(Bells Ad lib.)

*sub. mf*

55

ra - ga. _____             It was on - ly af - ter   dawn, _____

Wd. Blk.

*mf*

*sub. f*

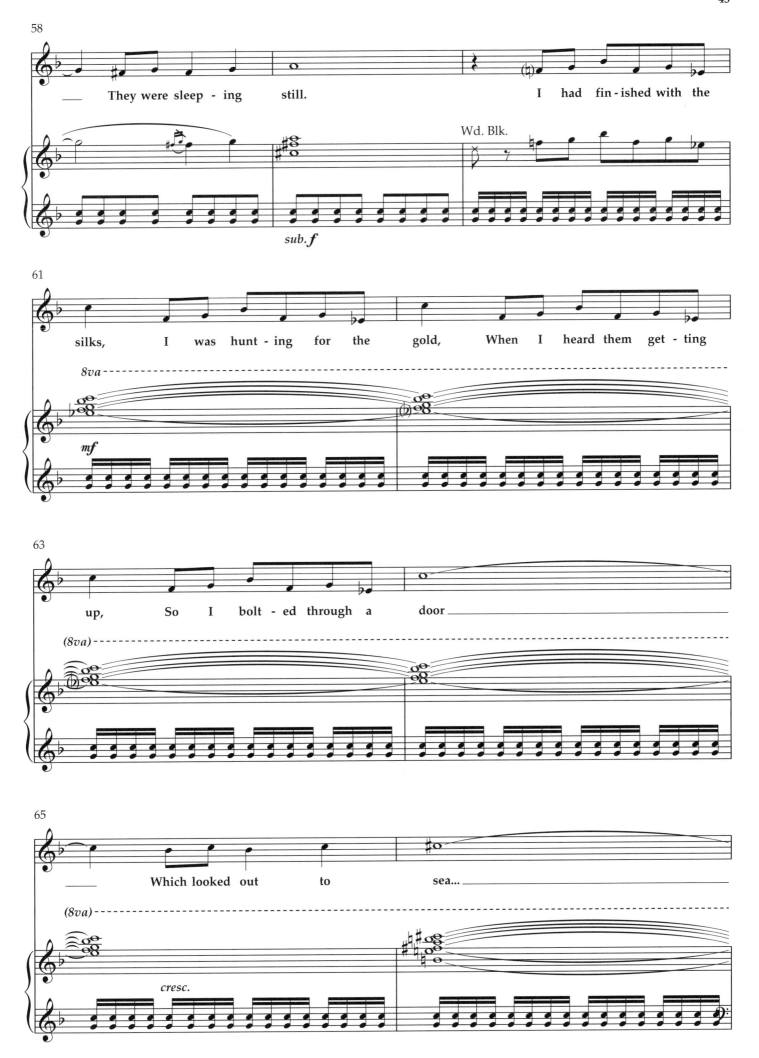

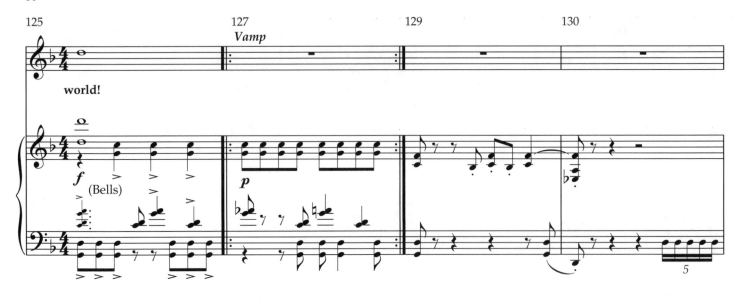

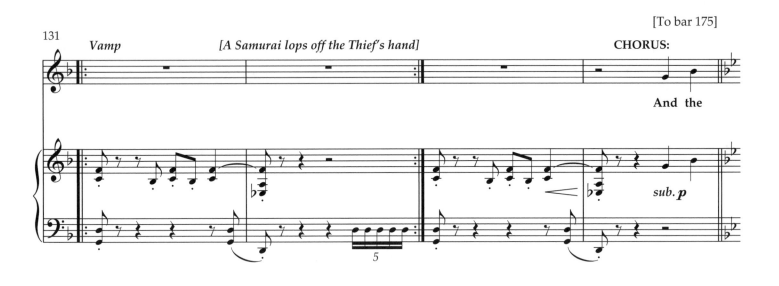

186 [repeat till exit]

(last time only)
RECITER:

188

[draws curtain]

And it    was.

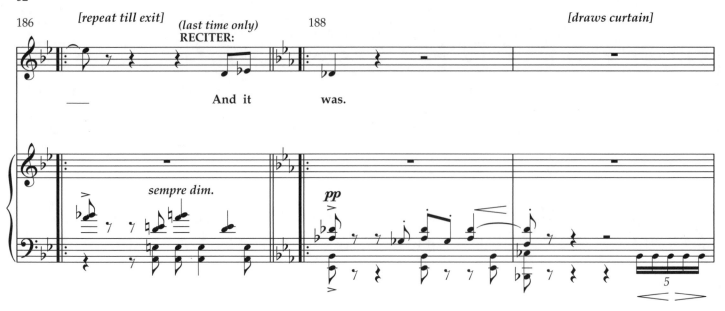

sempre dim.

pp

190

accel. e cresc. al Fine

192

sempre accel. e cresc.

194

ff

fff

8vb

# No. 5

# Chrysanthemum Tea

(Shogun's Mother, Shogun's Wife, Soothsayer, Priests,
Physician, Members of the Court)

1st Day

34

herb That's su - perb For dis - tur - banc - es at sea. Is the

36

Sho - gun feel - ing bet - ter? Good! Now what a - bout this let - ter? Is it

38

wise to de - lay, my lord? With the days dis - ap - pear - ing, Might we

41

ben - e - fit from hear - ing what the sooth - say - ers say, my lord?

O - ver here my lord...

**Più mosso**

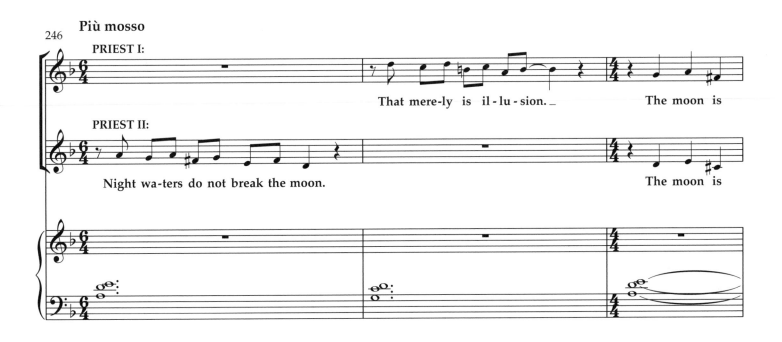

PRIEST I:

That mere-ly is il-lu-sion.___ The moon is

PRIEST II:

Night wa-ters do not break the moon. The moon is

sa-cred. That al-so is il-lu-sion.___

sa-cred. No for-eign ships can break our laws.

[To bar 301]

264

(Festival Drum)

301 3rd Day

WIFE:

Ah

305 MOTHER:

It's the day of the Ti - ger, my lord. On - ly

(WIFE:)

308 two days re - main - ing, And I'm ti - red of ex - plain - ing There are ships in the bay With a

Have some tea, my lord, Some chrys - an-the-mum tea. It's a

tan-gled sit - u - a -tion, As your fa -ther would a -gree. And it might -n't be so tan-gled If you

had -n't had him stran-gled— But I fear that I stray, my lord. I've a

nag - ging sus - pi - cion that in view of your con - di -tion, What we should do is pray, my

335

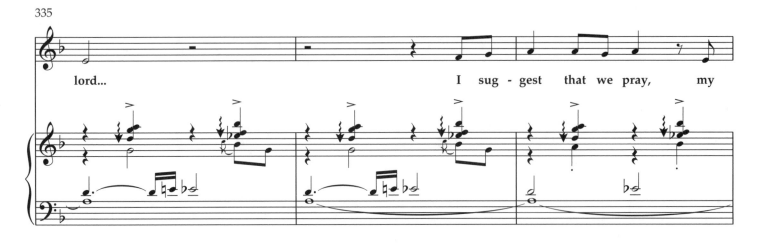

lord...                                        I sug - gest that we pray,    my

338

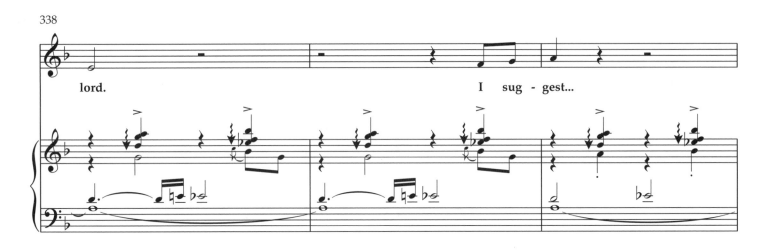

lord.                              I    sug - gest...

341

**SAMURAI COMPANION:**

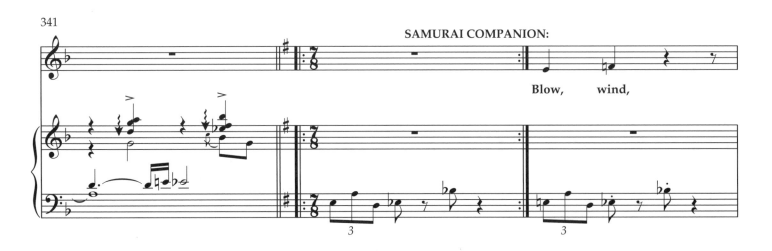

Blow,        wind,

344

great _ wind.        Great Ka - mi - ka - ze,        Wind of the gods.

362 **Marcato**

365

368 [To bar 401]

(Festival Drum)

401 **4th Day**

WIFE:

Ahh

417

My lord...

420

PHYSICIAN:

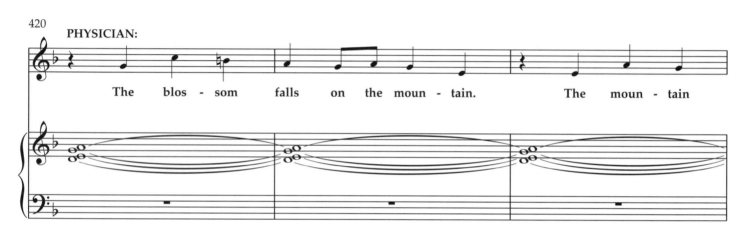

The blos - som falls on the moun - tain. The moun - tain

423

*rit.* *(Shogun twitches)* MOTHER:

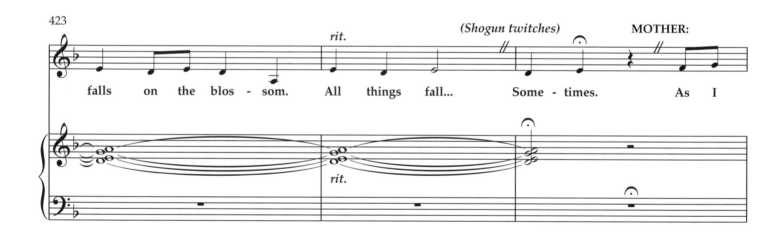

falls on the blos - som. All things fall... Some - times. As I

*rit.*

426

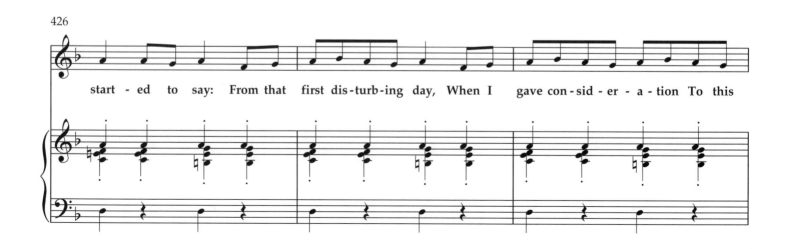

start - ed to say: From that first dis-turb-ing day, When I gave con-sid - er - a - tion To this

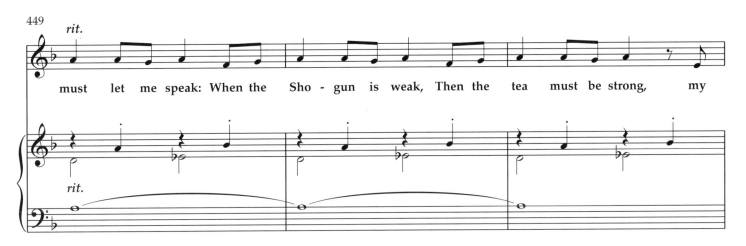

must let me speak: When the Sho - gun is weak, Then the tea must be strong, my

[He dies]

lord... My lord—?

**MOTHER (+PHYSICIAN):**

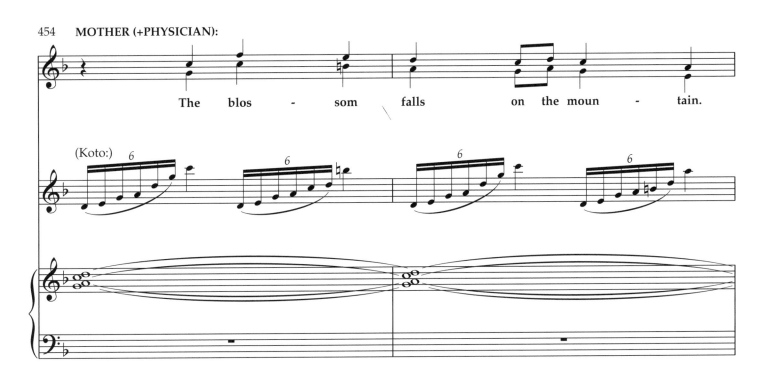

The blos - som falls on the moun - tain.

(Koto:)

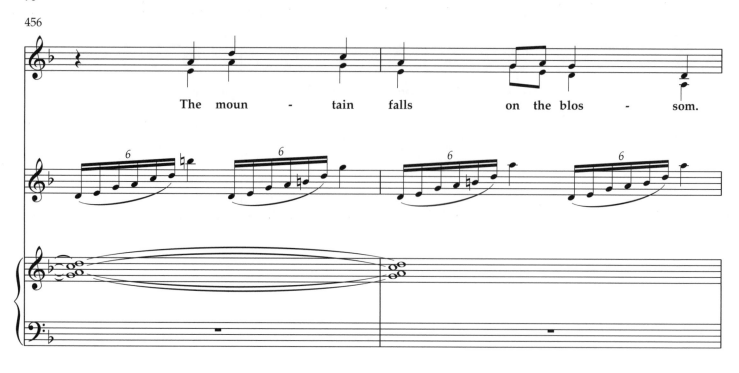

The moun - tain falls on the blos - som.

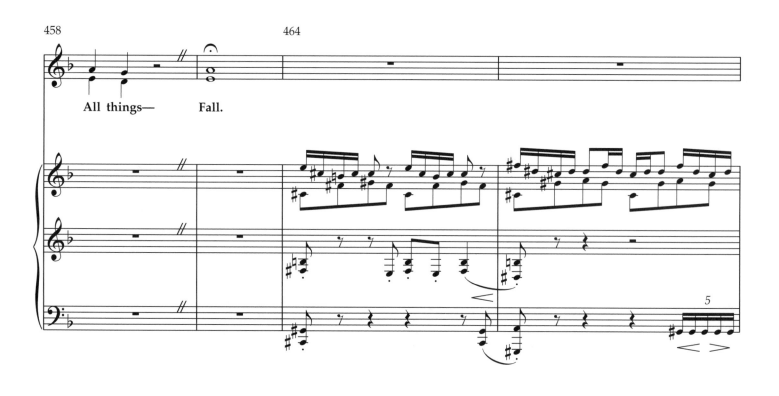

All things— Fall.

(Festival Drum)

# No. 5a

# Prayers - Underscore #2

*Cue:* **ABE: He is yours.**

**RECITER: If the Councilors can
no longer pretend...** *etc.*

*[Segue to No. 6 "Poems"]*

# No. 6

## Poems
### (Kayama, Manjiro)

*Cue:* **KAYAMA:** It is a long journey and we can keep each other company. I will make a poem.

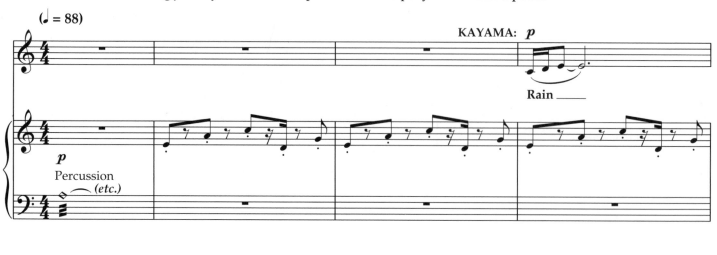

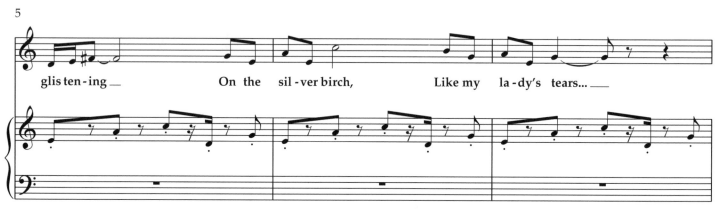

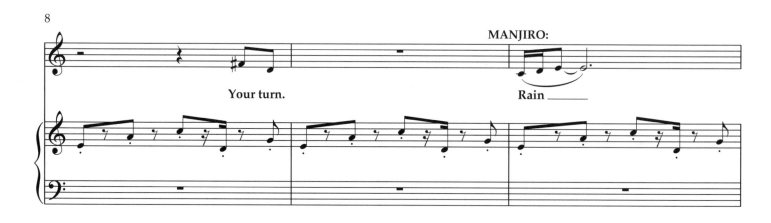

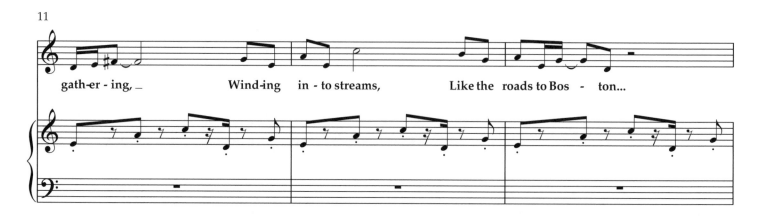

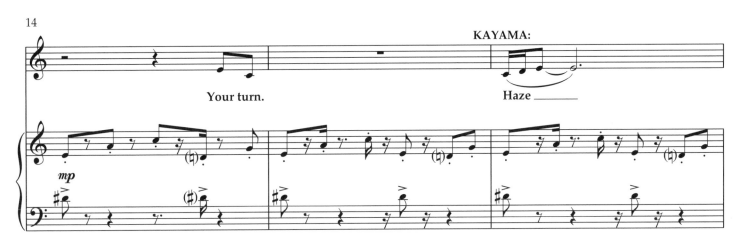

Your turn.                                        Haze _____

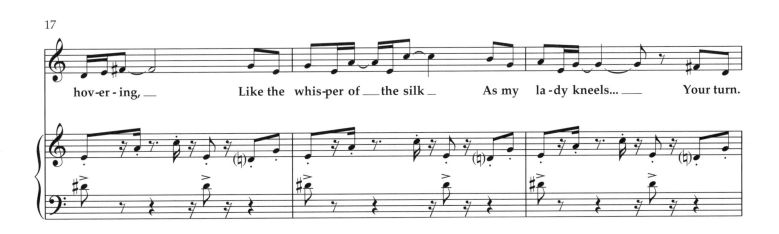

hov-er-ing, ___         Like the whis-per of ___the silk ___         As my    la-dy kneels... ___         Your turn.

Haze _____                                glit-ter-ing, ___                Like an

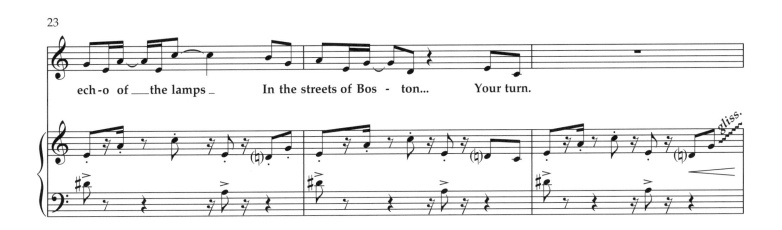

ech-o of ___the lamps ___         In the streets of Bos - ton...         Your turn.

26

KAYAMA:

Moon, _____ I love her like the moon, Mak - ing

28

jew - els of __ the grass __ Where my la - dy walks, _____ My la - dy wife...

30

MANJIRO:

Moon, _____ I love her like the moon, Wash - ing

32

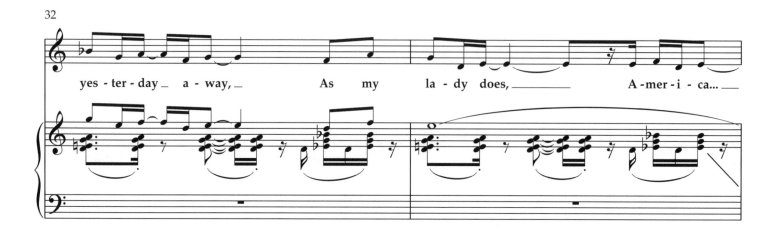

yes - ter - day __ a - way, __ As my la - dy does, _____ A - mer - i - ca...

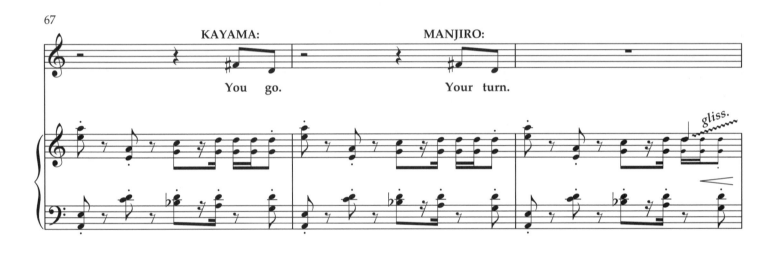

# No. 7 Welcome to Kanagawa
## (Madam, Four Girls, Reciter)

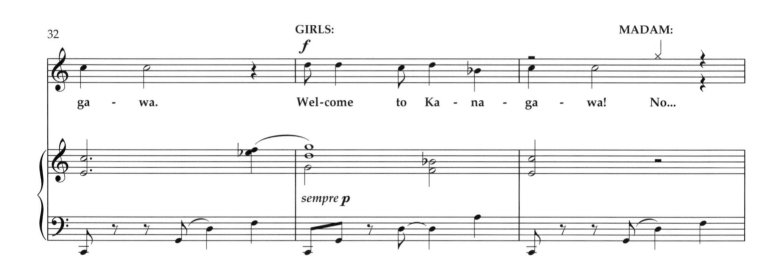

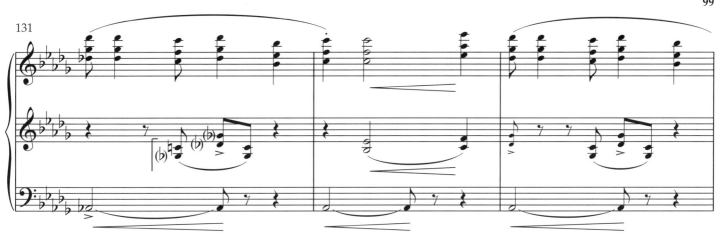

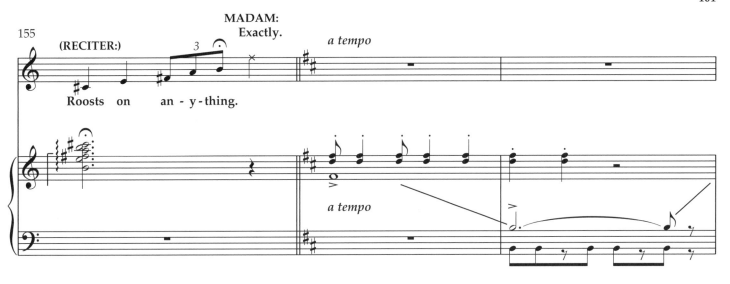

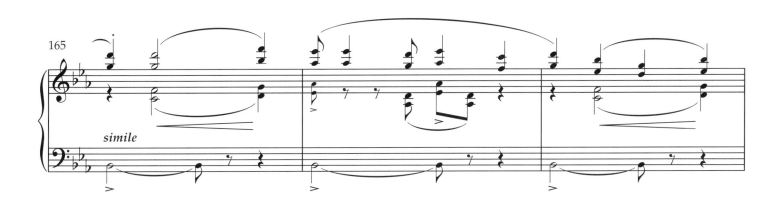

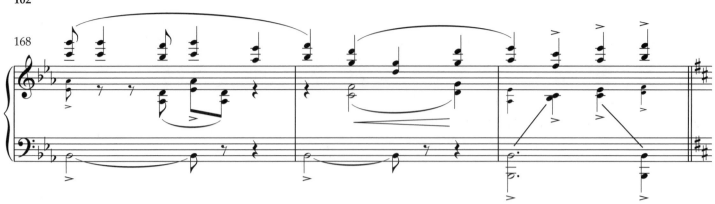

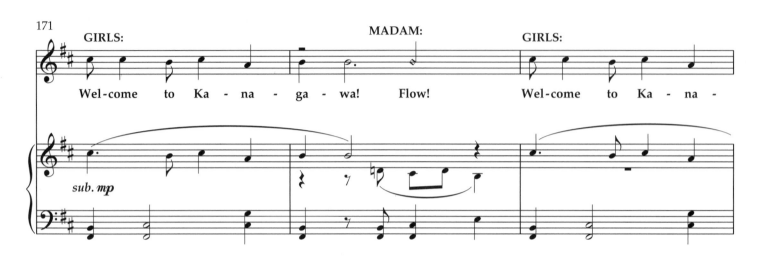

GIRLS:
Wel-come to Ka - na - ga - wa!

MADAM:
Flow!

GIRLS:
Wel-come to Ka - na -

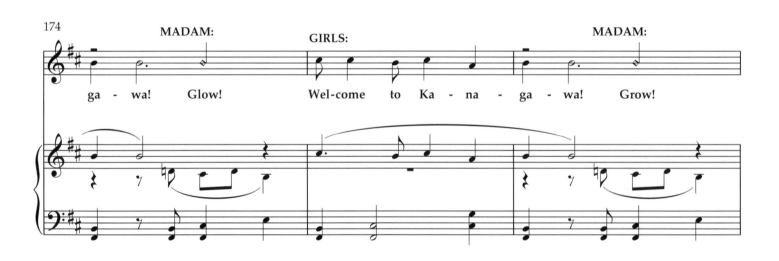

MADAM:
ga - wa! Glow!

GIRLS:
Wel-come to Ka - na - ga - wa!

MADAM:
Grow!

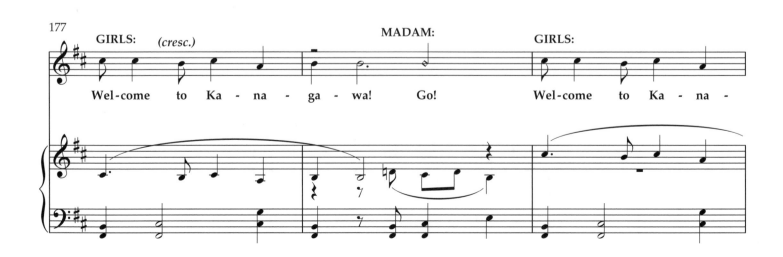

GIRLS: (cresc.)
Wel-come to Ka - na - ga - wa!

MADAM:
Go!

GIRLS:
Wel-come to Ka - na -

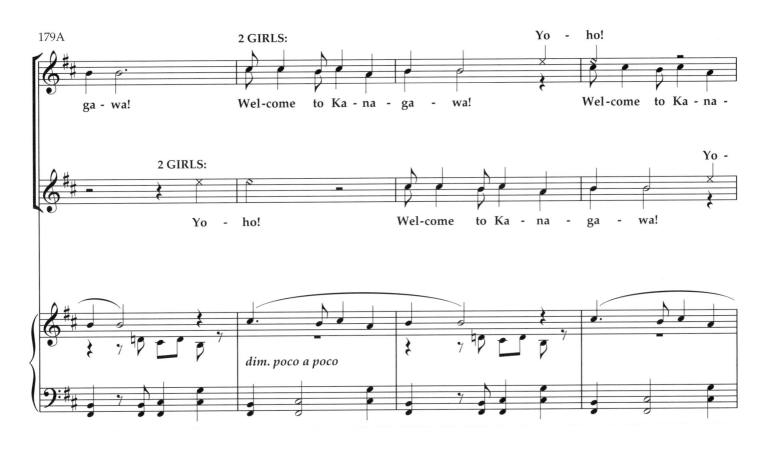

180

ga - wa.

184

188

GIRLS:

MADAM:

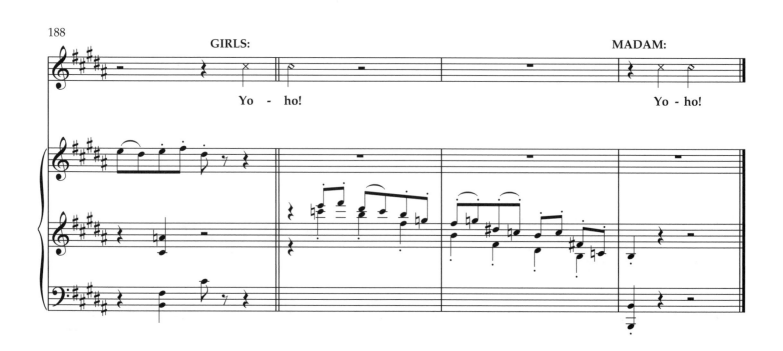

Yo - ho!

Yo - ho!

## Scene VIII

# No. 7a

*Entire scene accompanied by ad lib. military drum.*

## Scene X

# No. 7b

**RECITER:** From the personal journal of Commodore Matthew Perry... *etc.*
    *(accompanied by ad lib. military drum)*

*Cue:* **RECITER: ... by whatever means are necessary.**

# March to the Treaty House

# No. 7d

*Cue:* **COUNCILOR: Pity the Americans if they should draw their guns.**

# No. 8

# Someone in a Tree

## (Old Man, Reciter, Boy, Warrior)

*Cue:* RECITER: What a shame that there is no authentic Japanese account of what took place on that historic day.

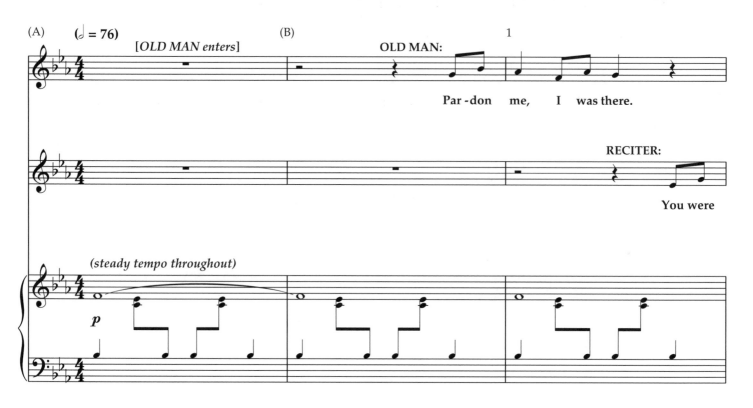

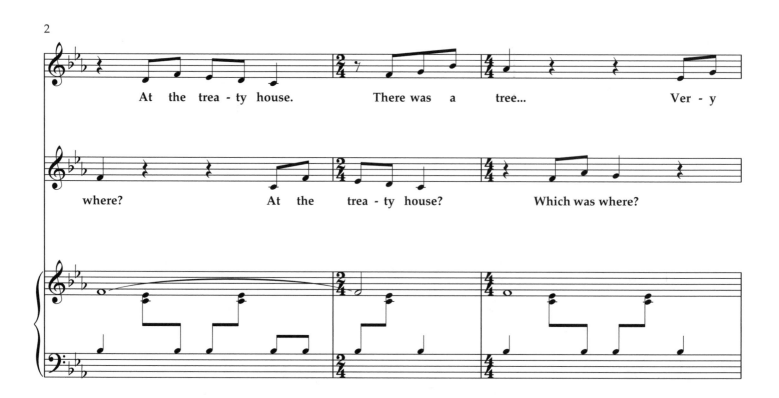

I was young - er then...

[A young boy appears]

BOY:

Tell him what I

OLD MAN:

see!

I am in a tree. I am ten.

I am in a tree.

267

(WARRIOR:)
want..." "Will you grant—?" "If you don't..." "We con-cede it..." I can Hear

OLD MAN:
And they Sat through the Night and they

BOY:

270

Them. I'm a Frag-ment of ___ the Day. ___ If I

Lit yel-low ta-pers. I was There Then. If I

And they Chat and they Fight and they Sit sign-ing Pa-pers. I am

273

(WARRIOR:)

(OLD MAN:)

(BOY:)

276

# No. 8a

# Incidental

*Cue:* RECITER: The Americans were satisfied and they left.

*Repeat until ABE says:* **Quickly there, nothing must remain.** *(Dialogue continues)*

Piccolo

*[Segue to No. 9 "Lion Dance"]*

# No. 9

# Lion Dance

*Cue:* **RECITER: The barbarian threat had forever been removed. Ha!**

[END ACT I]

# ACT II Prologue

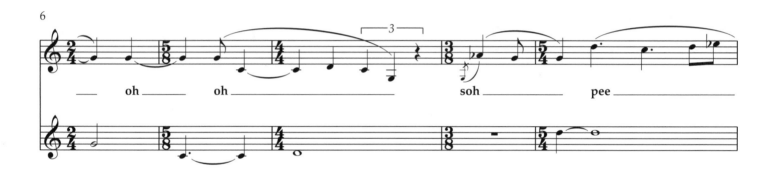

# No. 10

# Please Hello
## (Five Admirals)

*Cue:* ABE: Goodbye, Americans! Come back in two hundred fifty years!

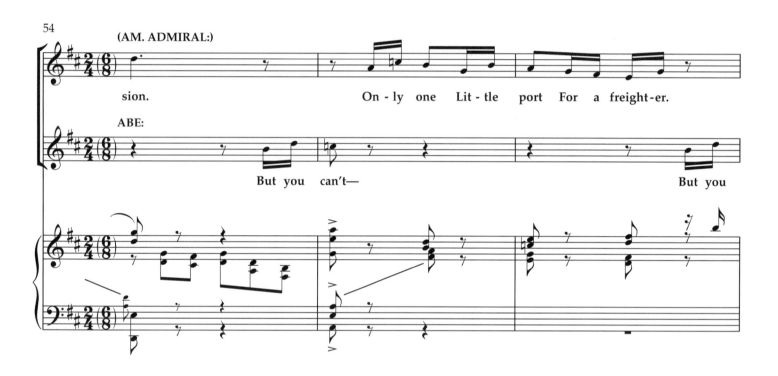

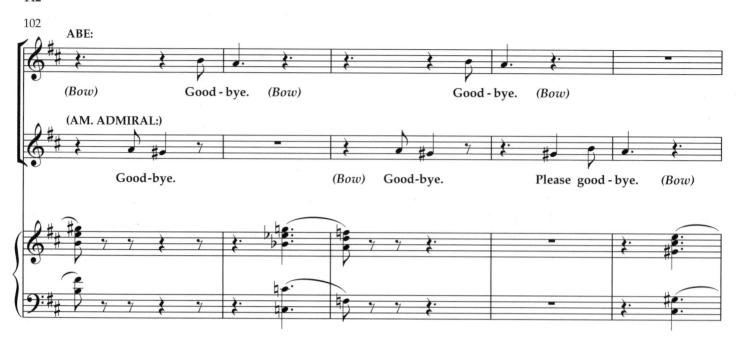

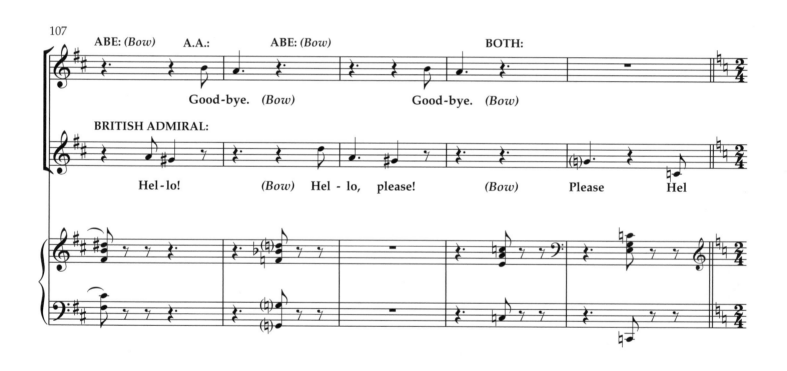

175

**Pesante**

DUTCH ADMIRAL:

Wait! Please hel - lo! Don't for - get the Dutch! Like to keep in touch.

*mp* heavily

178

Thank you ver - y much. Tell them to go,

182

But - ton up the lips. What do lit - tle Nips Want vit bat - tle-ships?

185

Hold ev - 'ry-thing, We gon - na bring

*cresc.*

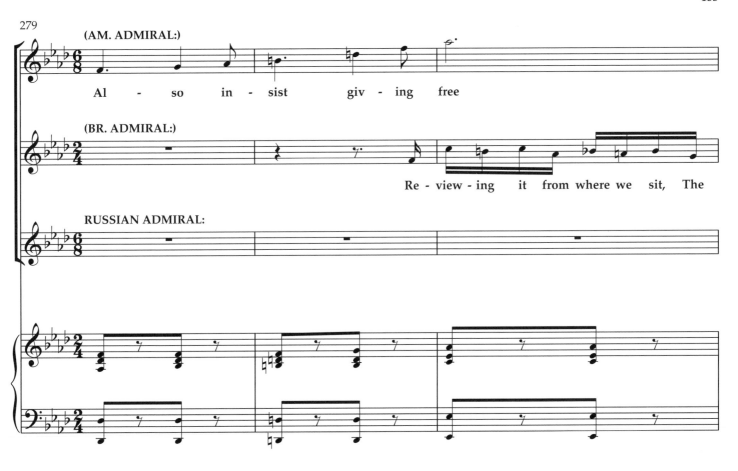

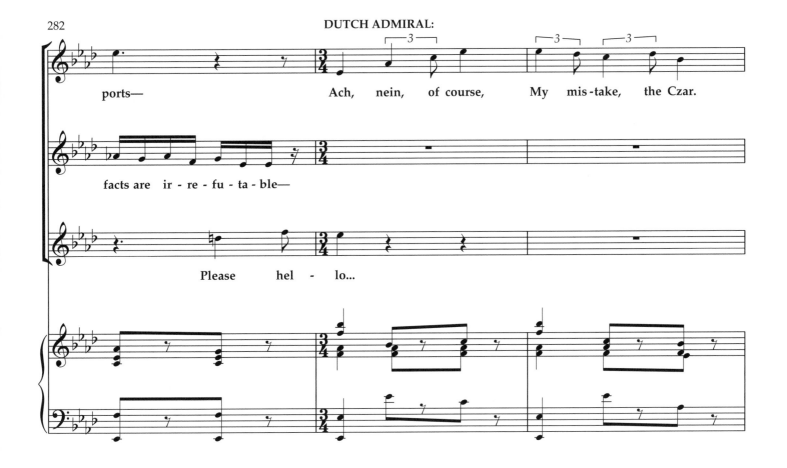

285

(DUT. ADMIRAL:)

AM. ADMIRAL:

Smell the cav - i - ar— Leave the door a - jar. Al - so want

(BR. ADMIRAL:)

(RUS. ADMIRAL:)

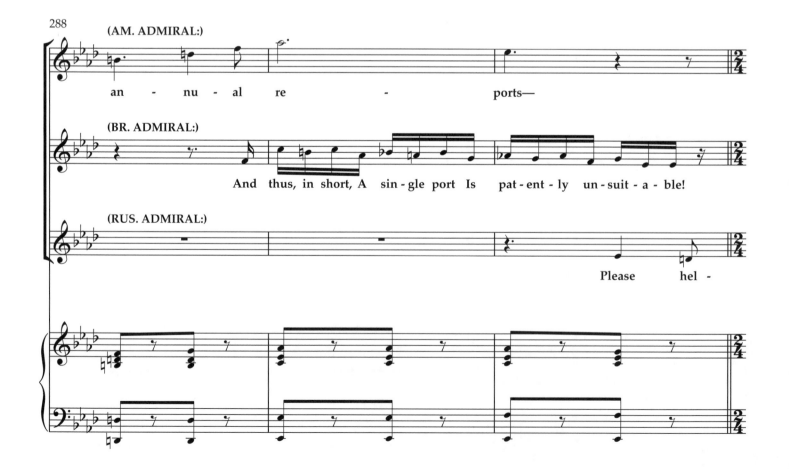

288

(AM. ADMIRAL:)

an - nu - al re - ports—

(BR. ADMIRAL:)

And thus, in short, A sin - gle port Is pat - ent - ly un - suit - a - ble!

(RUS. ADMIRAL:)

Please hel -

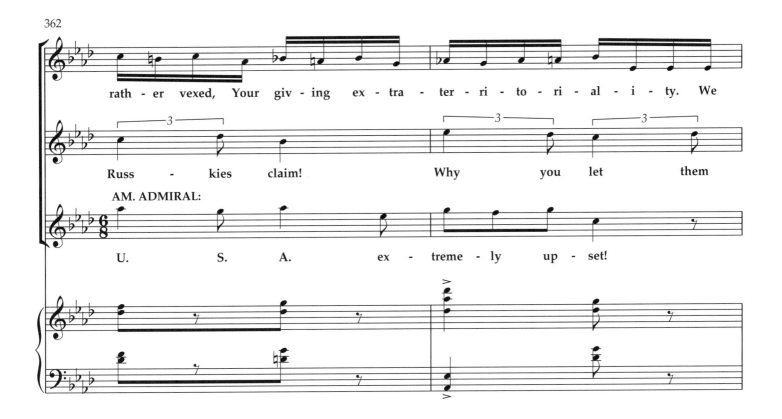

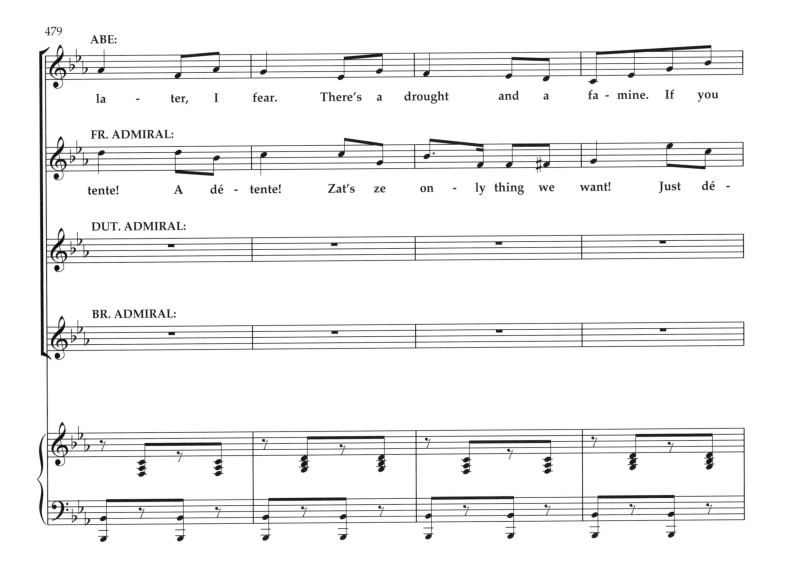

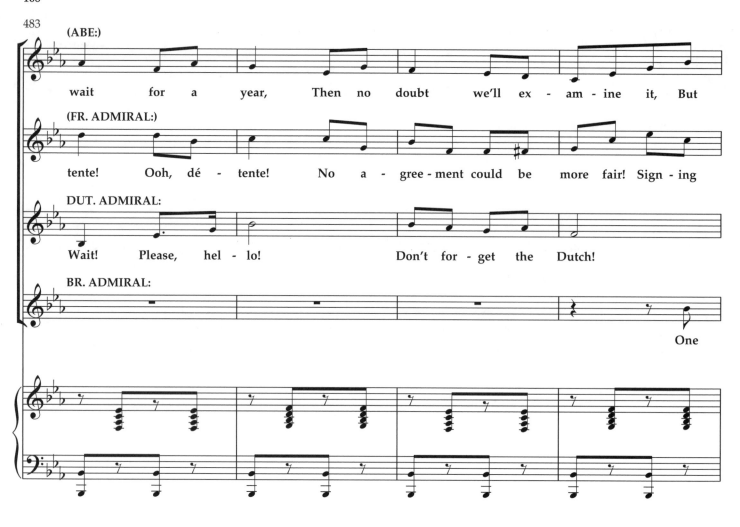

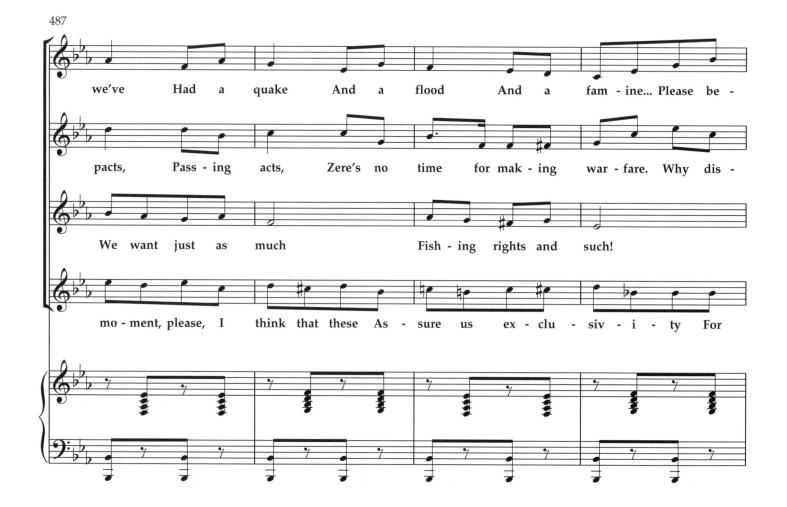

170

499

504

520
ALL:
lo! We must go, But our in - ter-course will grow Through dé -

524
tente, As dé - tente Brings com - plete co - op - er - a - tion. By the

528
way, may we say We a - dore your lit - tle na - tion, And with

532
heav - y can - non Wish you an un - end - ing please hel - lo!

*[Segue to No. 11 "Admirals' Playoff"]*

# No. 11

# ADMIRALS' PLAYOFF

(cont.)

# No. 12

# A Bowler Hat
### (Kayama, Manjiro, Reciter)

*Cue:* RECITER: A letter from Kayama Yesaemon to the Shogun.

*Reciter continues:* My Lord Abe. It is my privilege... *etc.*

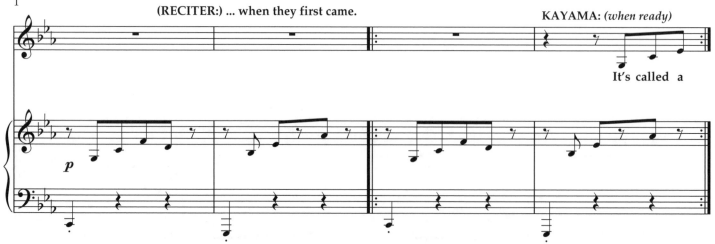

(RECITER:) ... when they first came.

KAYAMA: *(when ready)*

It's called a

21

milk be - fore the tea. _____ The Dutch am -

25

bas - sa - dor is no fool. _____ I must re -

29

mem - ber that. _____

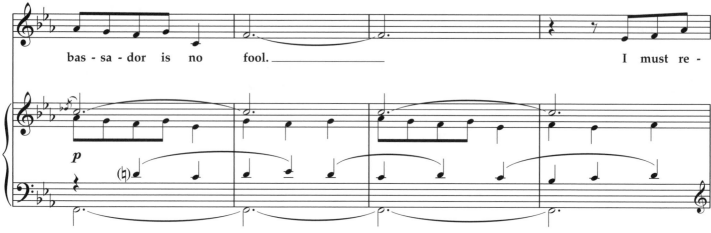

*Reciter reads:* **Three years ago we set one district...** *(cont.)*

33

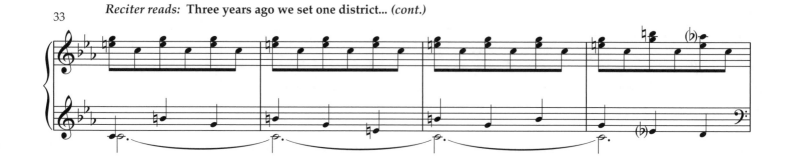

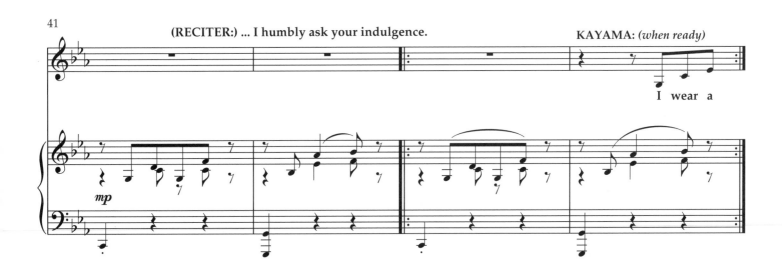

(RECITER:) ... I humbly ask your indulgence.

KAYAMA: *(when ready)*

I wear a

bow-ler hat.

They send me

wine. _____

The house is

*Reciter reads:* **Of all the westerners...** *etc.*

133

*Reciter reads:* **Although the westerners have...** *etc.*

137

*p*

141

145

(RECITER:) ... before entering the city.

KAYAMA:

I wind my

*mp*

149

pock-et watch.

We serve white

169

da - ble. _____

*p*

Where is my bow-ler hat?

dim.     *p*

174

*Reciter reads:* **I will not bother you with details...** *etc.*

(Shamisen)

(Shakuhachi)

*pp*

179

186

(RECITER:) ... only gentlemen may enter.

KAYAMA:

It's called a mon - o - cle.

I've left my wife. _____

No bird ex -

# No. 13

# Pretty Lady
(Three Sailors)

*Cue:* SAILOR: **What pretty flowers.**

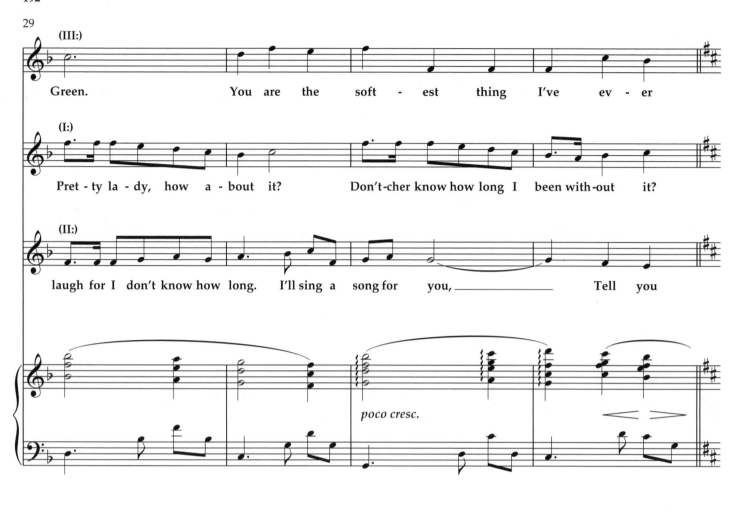

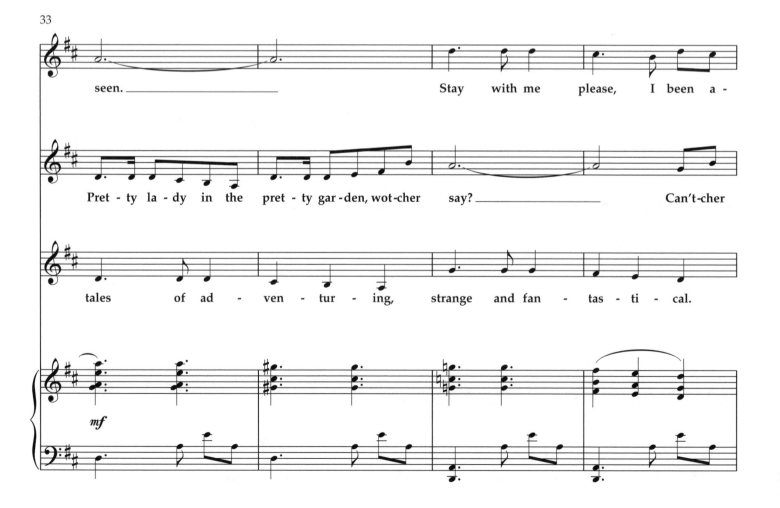

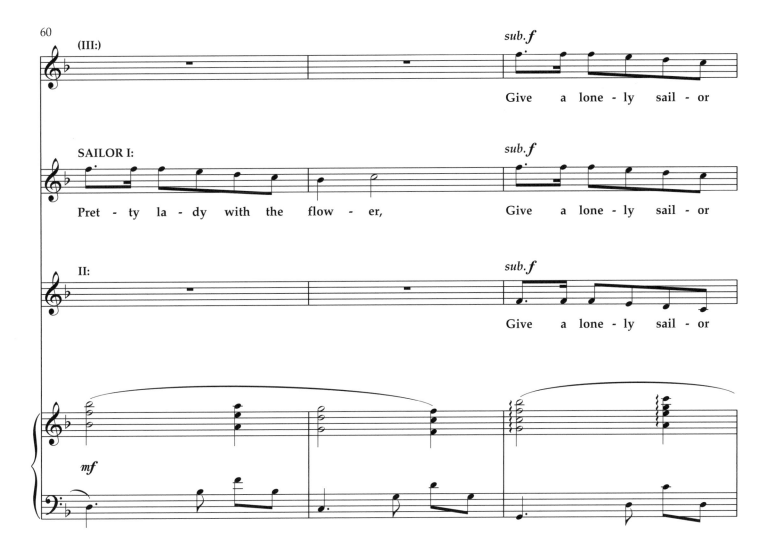

# No. 13a

# Royal Road

*Cue:* **RECITER: The Tokaido, the Royal Road from Edo to Kyoto.** *(cont. dialogue)*

*[On cue]*

[Shamisen plays under dialogue]

*On Cue:* **SAMURAI: Restore the Emperor!**　　　　　　　　　*Cue:* **CLOAKED FIGURE: Expel the Barbarians!**

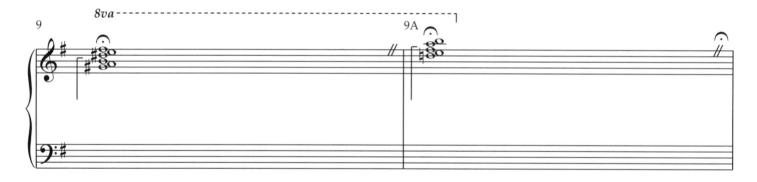

*Cue:* **KAYAMA: Conspirator—murderer—fisherman!**

# No. 14

# Next - Part I
## (Company)

*Cue:* RECITER/EMPEROR: ...eliminate all obstacles which hinder our development.

**Feroce** (♩ = 112)

*Reciter/Emperor continues:* We will organize an army... *etc.*

*mp*
[Play 6 times]
*f*

...what America has done for us!

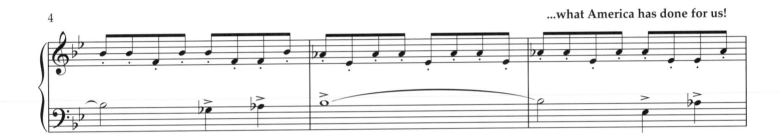

CHORUS:

Streams are flow - ing._____ See what's com - ing _____

RECITER/EMPEROR: We will build railroads, foundries, telegraphs and steamships.

[To bar 14]

Next!

R/E: Foreign architects will
reconstruct our cities.

CHORUS:

Next!

Wa - ters churn - ing,

Light - ning flash - es.

Kings are burn - ing,

Sift the ash - es—

R/E: The day will come when the western powers will be
forced to acknowledge us their undisputed equals.

[To bar 45]

Next!

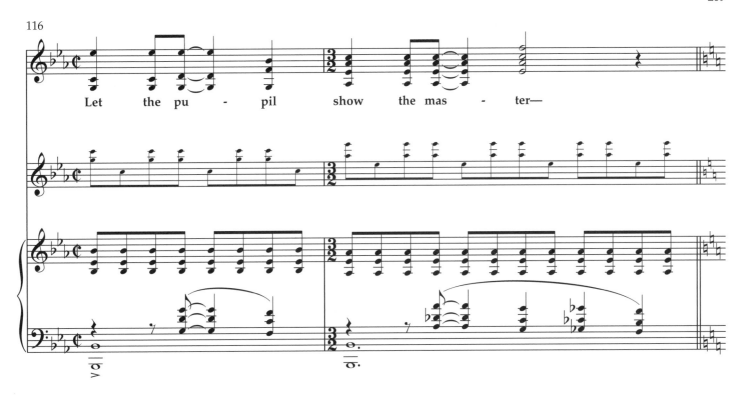

Let the pu - pil show the mas - ter—

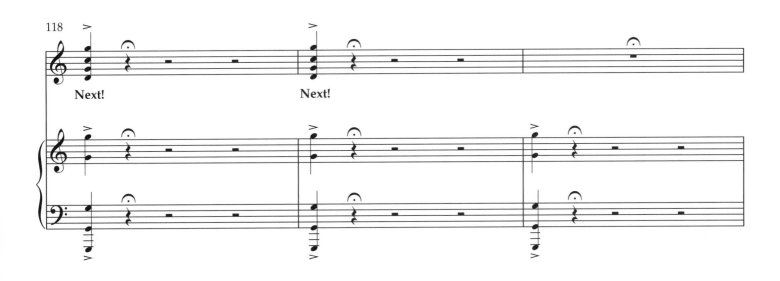

Next!

Next!

**A VOICE:** By 1965, there were 223 Japan Airline ticket offices in 199 cities throughout the world!

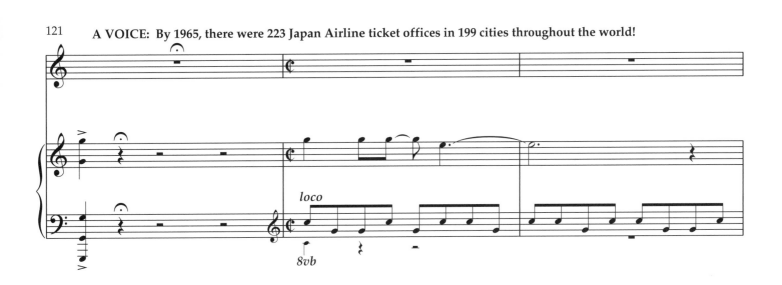

*loco*

*8vb*

FOURTH VOICE: The best-selling car in the United

States for the last 20 years has been the Toyota Camry!

213

# No. 14a

# Next - Part II

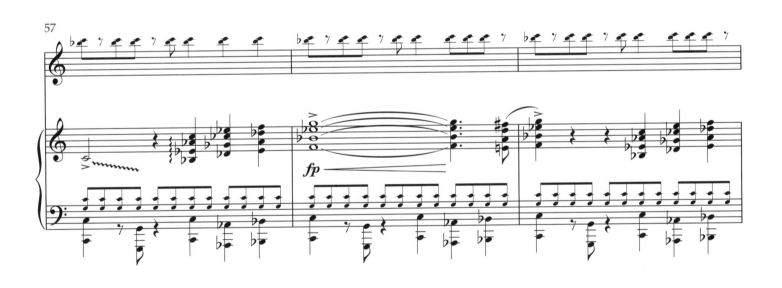

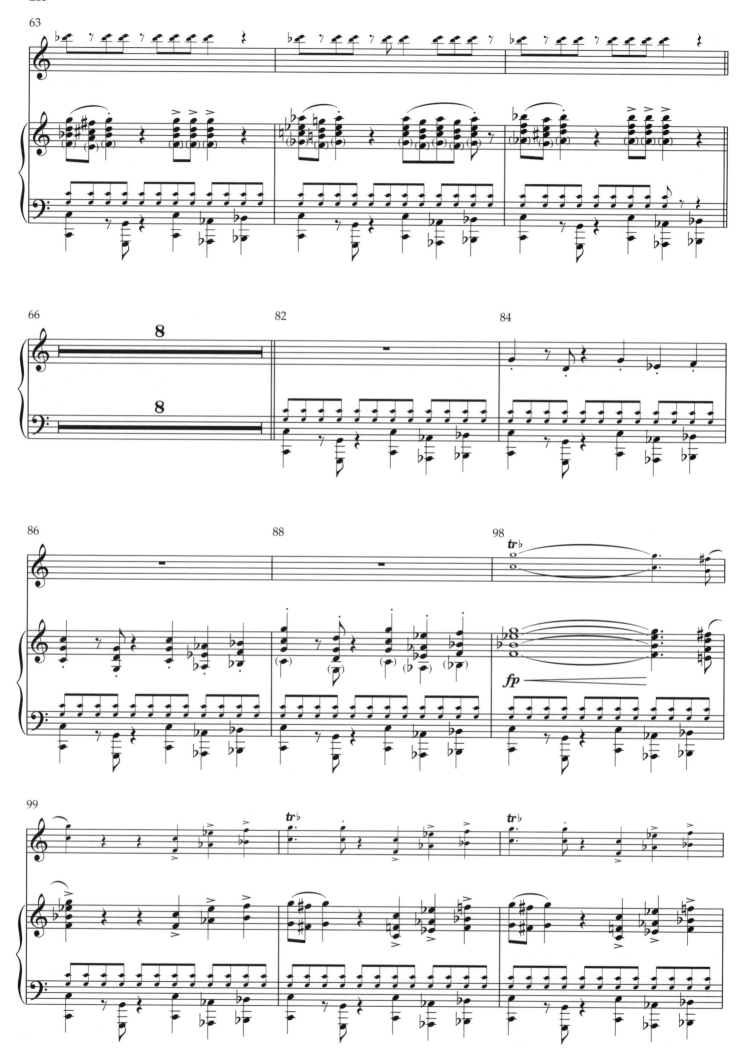

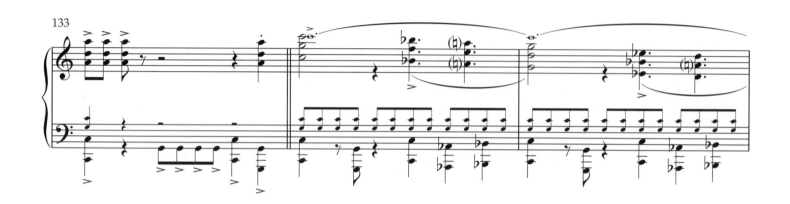

[To bar 35 - Part III]

RECITER: Nippon. The Floating Kingdom.

There was a time when foreigners were not welcome here.

But that was long ago. 130 years. (Pause) Welcome to Japan.

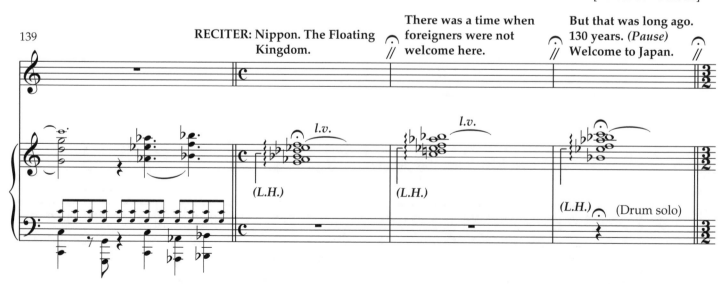

# No. 14b

# Next - Part III

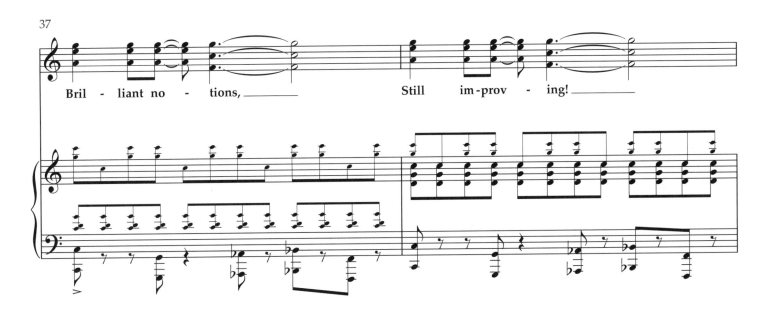

Make the mo - tions, _____ Keep it mov - ing— _____

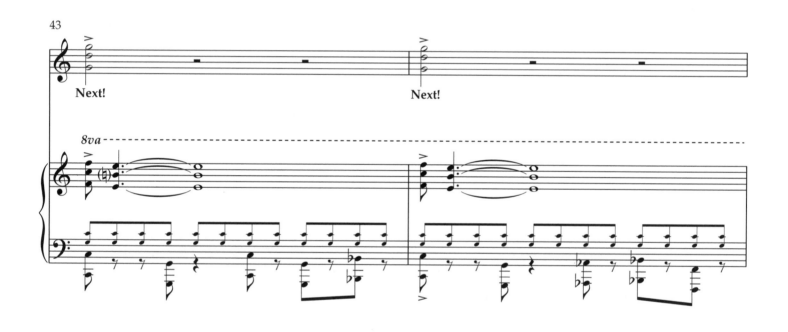

Next! Next!

Next!

[END ACT TWO]

# No. 15

# Exit Music

[To bar 126]

[Fine]